TULSA CITY-COUNTY LIBRARY

S0-AGK-044

Tell Me Why

WHY?

Dolphins Breathe Air

Susan H. Gray

Published in the United States of America by Cherry Lake Publishing
Ann Arbor, Michigan
www.cherrylakepublishing.com

Content Adviser: Dr. Stephen S. Ditchkoff, Professor of Wildlife Sciences, Auburn University,
Auburn, Alabama
Reading Adviser: Marla Conn, Readability, Inc.

Photo Credits: © PathDoc/Shutterstock Images, cover, 1, 7; © michaeljung/Shutterstock Images, cover, 1, 19;
© xavier gallego morell/Shutterstock Images, cover, 1, 17; © Willyam Bradberry/Shutterstock Images, cover,
1, 7, 15 ; © Christian Musat/Shutterstock Images, cover, 1; © Kristina Vackova/Shutterstock Images, cover,
1; © fotografie4you/Shutterstock Images, 5; © Dai Mar Tamarack/Shutterstock Images, 9; © Debra
McGuire/Thinkstock, 11; © KKulikov/Shutterstock Images, 13; © PedroMatos/Shutterstock Images, 15;
© Tory Kallman/Dreamstime.com, 19; © Palis Michalis/Shutterstock Images, 21

Copyright ©2015 by Cherry Lake Publishing
All rights reserved. No part of this book may be reproduced or utilized in any form or by any means
without written permission from the publisher.

Library of Congress Cataloging-in-Publication Data

Gray, Susan Heinrichs, author.
  Dolphins breathe air / Susan H. Gray.
     pages cm. -- (Tell me why)
  Summary: "Young children are naturally curious about animals. Dolphins
Breathe Air offers answers to their most compelling questions about how
these mammals can swim. Age-appropriate explanations and appealing photos
encourage readers to continue their quest for knowledge. Additional text
features and search tools, including a glossary and an index, help students
locate information and learn new words."—Provided by publisher.
  Audience: Ages 6-10.
  Audience: K to grade 3.
  Includes bibliographical references and index.
  ISBN 978-1-63188-991-2 (hardcover) -- ISBN 978-1-63362-030-8 (pbk.) --
ISBN 978-1-63362-069-8 (pdf) -- ISBN 978-1-63362-108-4 (ebook) 1.
Dolphins--Juvenile literature. 2. Dolphins--Respiration--Juvenile
literature. 3. Dolphins--Physiology--Juvenile literature. 4. Children's
questions and answers. I. Title.

QL737.C432G723 2015
599.53--dc23

                   2014031831

Cherry Lake Publishing would like to acknowledge the work of The Partnership for 21st Century Skills.
Please visit www.21.org for more information.

Printed in the United States of America
Corporate Graphics

Table of Contents

Alyssa's Questions 4

Life in the Sea 8

A Hole in the Head 12

The Dolphin's Relatives 18

Think About It 22

Glossary 23

Find Out More 23

Index 24

About the Author 24

Alyssa's Questions

Alyssa and her family were on vacation. They were on a big boat with lots of people. Everyone was watching for dolphins.

"There they are!" Alyssa shouted. She waved her hands and pointed. Everyone turned to look. Dolphins were leaping from the water.

A man in a uniform came over to Alyssa. "You were really paying attention," he said. "You would make a good scientist someday."

Most dolphins live in oceans all around the world.

Alyssa's eyes lit up. She loved the ocean. And she loved animals. She wanted to ask the man about dolphins.

"I know dolphins are not fish," she began. "But what are they? Do they only live in the ocean? How do they breathe?" She was full of questions.

The man laughed. "One question at a time, please," he said. Then he began to talk about dolphins. Everyone moved in closer so they could hear.

Ask your classmates what they know about dolphins. See if anyone thinks a dolphin is a fish.

Dolphins live in the water, but they are not fish.

Life in the Sea

"Some **species** of dolphins live in rivers," the man began. "But most live in the ocean. They spend their days swimming, playing, and eating. They love to eat fish, squid, and shrimp.

"Dolphins travel in groups called pods," he continued. "Sometimes, a pod works together to feed. First, members of the pod surround some fish. The fish quickly become trapped. Then it is easy for the dolphins to catch them."

Dolphins work together when hunting.

The man went on. "Dolphins are **mammals**. Cows, dogs, bears, and people are also mammals. Like all other mammals, dolphins have lungs. They breathe air, just like we do. Fish, however, have gills. Gills make it possible to breathe underwater. Dolphins do not have gills."

Alyssa was confused. She knew dolphins spent their lives in the water. So how do they get the air they need? She waited for the man to explain.

Both dolphins and humans have lungs.

A Hole in the Head

Alyssa's question was soon answered. The man pointed out that a dolphin may look like it has a nose or snout for breathing. But, it has a blowhole instead. This is a single hole on the top of the animal's head. It leads to a tube called the **trachea**, or windpipe. The trachea carries air to the dolphin's lungs.

When a dolphin breathes in, air comes into the blowhole. It moves down the windpipe and to the lungs. Air moves out through the same pathway.

Dolphins breathe through a hole in their head called a blowhole.

A flap covers the blowhole. Muscles control the flap. When the muscles tighten up, the flap opens. When they relax, it closes. Once the flap is shut, water cannot leak in.

As a dolphin comes to the surface, its blowhole opens. The dolphin **exhales**. Next, the dolphin quickly **inhales**. Then its blowhole clamps shut. Breathing out and in takes less than half a second!

Dolphins must come to the water's surface to breathe air.

A dolphin cannot breathe through its mouth. The mouth just leads to the stomach. Only the blowhole leads to the lungs. This design protects the dolphin. Its airway does not get blocked by food. A dolphin with a fish in its throat can still breathe. And dolphins will not choke on water while trying to eat.

What if a dolphin had gills? Would it need a blowhole?

This goldfish breathes through gills instead of a blowhole.

The Dolphin's Relatives

Dolphins are related to whales and **porpoises**. Most of these animals live in the ocean. All of them are mammals. So they all breathe air. And they all have blowholes.

When they exhale, sometimes it makes a spray of water. This water is not from their lungs. It is the ocean water that is just above their blowholes.

LOOK!

This whale is using its blowhole. Is it inhaling or exhaling?

Like dolphins, whales have blowholes and lungs.

There are some great places to see dolphins up close. You might see them at a **marine** park or zoo. Better yet, you can watch dolphins in the ocean. Large boats often take people out to look for dolphins. You might see them swimming next to the boat. Or you might spot them leaping from the water. What a fun way to learn more about these amazing animals!

A marine park or zoo can be a good place to learn about dolphins.

Think About It

Dolphins can hold their breath underwater for more than 10 minutes. How is this helpful when they are feeding?

Why do dolphins have to breathe out and in so quickly?

Dolphins can breathe air. So why can't they just live on land?

Glossary

exhales (ex-HAYLZ) breathes out

inhales (in-HAYLZ) breathes in

mammals (MAM-uhlz) animals that breathe air and that produce milk for their babies

marine (muh-REEN) having to do with the sea

porpoises (POR-puh-suzz) air-breathing animals similar to dolphins but with shorter snouts

species (SPEE-sheez) types or kinds of living things

trachea (TRAY-kee-uh) the tube that carries air to and from the lungs

Find Out More

Books:

Arlon, Penelope. *Dolphins*. Danbury, CT: Scholastic, 2014.

Harris, Caroline. *Whales and Dolphins*. New York: Kingfisher, 2010.

Stewart, Melissa. *Dolphins*. Washington, DC: National Geographic Children's Books, 2010.

Web Sites:

Enchanted Learning—Dolphins
http://www.enchantedlearning.com/themes/dolphins.shtml
This site includes a quiz about dolphins, a dolphin body printout to label body parts, and much more.

Kids' Cruz—Dolphins: Breathing, Sleeping
www.kidscruz.com/DOL_BS.HTM
Visit this page for some interesting facts about dolphins and how they breathe.

National Geographic Kids—Bottlenose Dolphin
http://kids.nationalgeographic.com/content/kids/en_US/animals/bottlenose-dolphin
Here you can click through links to a dolphin video, game, and information about how dolphins communicate.

Index

air, 10, 12, 14, 15, 18, 22

blowhole, 12, 13, 14, 18, 19
breathing, 10, 12, 13, 14, 15, 16, 18, 22

dolphins
  where they live, 8

eating, 8, 16, 22
exhaling, 14

food, 8, 16

gills, 10, 17

head, 12
hunting, 9

inhaling, 14

lungs, 10, 11, 12, 16, 19

mammals, 10, 18
mouth, 16
muscles, 14

pods, 8

stomach, 16

trachea, 12

About the Author

Susan H. Gray has a master's degree in zoology. She has worked in research and has taught college-level science classes. Susan has also written more than 140 science and reference books, but especially likes to write about animals. She and her husband, Michael, live in Cabot, Arkansas, with many pets.